the kentucky rules

the kentucky rules

Cynthia Nelson

drawings by Tara Jane O'Neil

Soft Skull Press

1998

Acknowledgements
photo by Noel Brather Hawley
thank you Maggie Nelson for editorial assistance
thank you Letitia Quesenberry & Bea Chambers
thank you Mia Frederick & Greta Ritcher
& Steven Thornton
thank you Louisville friends
©1998 Cynthia Nelson
illustrations ©1998 Tara Jane O'Neil

the kentucky rules

I. always say fly south

II. gypsying

I. always say fly south

west virginia pearls

stealing kisses from the road, not folks
& driving like a champion a girl who is hoarse
fumes putrid & uncompromising pouring into
this compartment, through a window lost
shattered by a bullet of boredom
the west virginia peaks challenge our motors
still the champion the fine companion
lets me shine inside & out

we're packing oil paintings from '57 & '59
couldn't bear to throw them out, guess it's
preferable to paint over them with respect
there's disabled amplifiers to be delivered
to a land of greater space & less stress
debted & crumbling road cases holding
memories, german aromas, wild dreams
of previous owners, all of which led them
to sell the whole shebang
in rochester new york in 1988
i purchased the amps in cases
i guess that it (looks like i)
purchased the dreams

i'm going back to my cemeteries
to wasteland walks & wantonness
trips chiseled out of calendars
& hand-held mementos
my momentary loneliness eclipsed by a kiss
lips not dangerous but generous
checking in on me, my bliss at the desk
crisp wisdoms at the fingertips
steady decisions of aesthetic being made
me in the sunshine palace, my room with a bed
peace at the hand of no day job, no babysitting

the plastic's flapping on that shot-out window
distributing ghetto jewels on various grounds & gravels
i've got drumming blisters
worn treads/used sneakers
from flat-footed tennis players
who practiced every day
as we drive real fast past a funeral by the freeway
dreaming the songs we make, the last communiqué

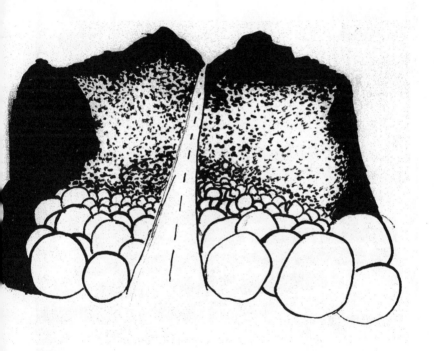

goddard avenue (autumn version)

there is nowhere to go that is polite
the lights are out, our questions dark
cut hair on the mint green sink
bathrooms are boundless, indigenous

when soup is on, she made it
the snipped hair is hers, the snores

we beg time apart, wear our p.j.'s thin
accepting goosebumps as glamour
we categorize

the flutter in her lungs sounds like owls' wings
the mists in mine are frank

feet get chilled, hairs fall out, thumbs scar
mincemeat season we dug out the pumpkin
after walking past mansions spotting
which ones were haunted

hearing, control, blinders

we have a scent
melody on the breath
a parade of symphonics

i asked for you
used my voice
insistent as a song
as an oak leaf on the floor

this is our last day together
you know how it goes
i was sent
to tell you this
you know
how it
goes

patience
inside patience, lust
listen
i can't really hear i can't
concentrate
i was painting & it made me
high
i'm trying to listen to what
you're doing
your (open A) montage in the heat

you've been making me something
to take home
i respect you, your admissions
i admit you, admit i love you
arrive lugging pockets
of our enigmatic cough

you broke a string
the snare must not stop
& i will not faint

coffee
i poured
what i couldn't finish in
the gutter
where you sometimes sleep
where you blend
where i have blended & hesitated

fancy hickey
i gave you it
not a postcard
you use your hearing
mine is thin
my back aches
our hunches
your hip

i revere you
you're dignified
not high half the time
real spoon not plastic
real time

divine
it's ok to say divine
losing the light
aware of the savior
of what we are making
when we stab at a pastry
hooves on

divine
it's ok to say divine
i noticed that the fridge was open
i noticed napkins
invented sky
big & blue and aware of blue
you & inner thigh

i believe in you
& i'll do you no wrong
i address you
& i'll address you in song

feverish

a little bit of lore in the night

instead of eloping we swig
& the lady who was mean
to you in the deli
haunts you

during the movie you wore
a black leather cowboy hat
we made out like
gypsies

you are coming here permanently so soon
with autumn in tow i can see it now
"i love you, good morning, let's do a day"
"meet you at the bar at 7, otherwise
your shoe"

pssst, hey bandit
big & purple like fruit
there's so many words
but let's make more
let's be vulnerable
in our robes
good for us

snooze

the alarm makes the same sound every 9 minutes
& you & i rotate like rotisserie chickens
cooking in bed juice upon skewers of sleep

i'm always done before you, meat sliding off
& you cry out hold me, hold onto me, someplace

cave hill cemetery

2 mini marts
4 lanes crossed
she fell asleep
beside a headstone

3 mini marts
still seeking matches
4 lanes crossed
looking for swans

calvary cemetery

hard-earned plots on hilltops
roots of the maple try
to squeeze out a headstone
like a man out of thighs

running in circles
on decrepit knees
away from dogs

squirrels are lean
conquest: nuts
dead telephone operators
one named marie

flies are rampant
they chopped down a tree
i suppose it was dying

imagine dream time permanente
in the sleek & windy hills

there are fits to feel
one or two exits
imagined pursuit by other mourners

it's not right to chase rainbows there
some greedy would-be ravens
would-be pigeons & crows

this wispy site over which planes fly
military ones, & the dead there lie

lesbian bitches

lying down crying clutching
two dollar bills, so moved by
drawn pictures of the moon

crawling into bed this morning
with the magic word cramps
automatic comfort in our world

we were holding hands when
a kid yelled lesbian bitches from the
schoolbus which is so high up

i was proud of her, she yelled
"who's teaching you that?"
& grabbed her tits for them

but a bus can be a getaway
& maybe they
will never learn

that a woman is an ocean
full of tides & tired lives
murmurs, & daily murders

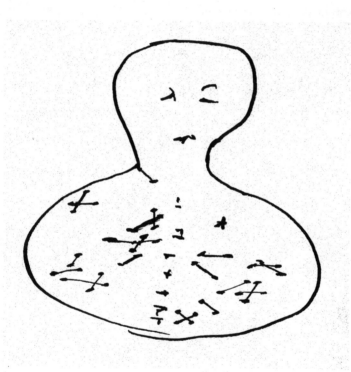

we could be anywhere

we could be anywhere but there's clues that we're not. our cars all covered in snow for one. if we're anywhere well then how did we get there. number two you're in bed with an unnamed ailment. from time to time you get them, no coffee for you, none of your favorite cheese, i have to eat double and lie very close to you. at night you feel better and so consume liquor and cigarettes. the trees are all bare. how i hate the seasons. the sunlight is thin and i've no use for a gazebo in a blizzard.

so anyway we're here. i like it here. i like being here with you. i wish you would feel better. since we don't know what's wrong with you, i get you to describe what it feels like. "bad" is too vague so i urge you further. you always mention bones and blood and that you feel like you're dying. i know that you're scared so i remain calm. the doctors never know what's wrong with you either so we wait it out. worst case scenarios i keep to myself. like the one where you're in the hospital and i'm distraught so i have to tell your parents that i'm in love with you, and they forbid me to see you. because you don't need to think about that, you need to receive the health vibes i am sending. get well my magic sweetheart. you are such an amazing self. like when you're three-dimensional dancing and yelling crazy things. even though i am always in bed with you i can't quite get to know your insides, confusing the details of your medical history, tonsils for bladders, steroids for morphines, exotic tiger scars of an ambition called the will to live.

we live here in this house. a house is something surrounded by a lot of air. no people live in the house that you don't know. you are responsible for garbage and recycling. you are responsible for waking up and making something of yourself. you are responsible for your past lives, keeping them alive for good reasons and/or editing them. you can see the sky and it is responsible for sunlight and rain. you can send your messages via telecommunications. you can watch people choosing lime or a lemon to chase their tequila. you can wish you had a kitchen table, but then there's always something that you don't have. you can forget that the barren tree is a peach tree and that mosquitoes were once on the pond.

right now there is lint in my hair for i am not responsible for washing it, for bathing my body or dancing in the bar. yet i do these things, i buy 65 cent snack mix at deddens' highland fling. this is where we imbibe quite cheaply. it is its own poem, located here and for what. the whiskey sours and the wind chimes. you have a pretty green vial, but the pills in it do not suffice. they do not specify "take when bones and blood feel wrong." i speak cheerful psalms and my version of prayers. and the sun she is moving across my page.

good at

i myself am not eloquent about the darkness
i am good at saving phrases & moments in time
hyperventilation & motivation
skimming cream off the tops of bready desserts
making 2% out of skim & half & half
hanging a wet towel artfully off a door
radiating nervousness
raising & lowering the shades
sitting watch over a flood
in a new town where the river rises
where i hear the river rising
& the baby crying
is not mine

waiting

to whine is not to feel better
cognac warms her throat to excess
she longs to be the zombie of the day

she's not living, only saying a few things
treason is to drop out, also to drop back in
trying to tell the truth which takes too long

same bar, different town
always waiting for some season to come around
today she made a brilliant breakfast, arms flying

she keeps to herself, trudging through snows
what's so wonderful about her efforts
when nobody has time to write her back?

big-boned & burdened by her intellect
thinking, "you really can't know, can you?"
&, "there really is no sense now, is there?"

waiting to begin anything is actually terrible
she's compared her notions to the elders'
& on this one they comply

if the city is a girl

if the city is a girl, you are married to her; you are married to a wiser woman than most. her hair has roots that are stronger & divided by a straighter line. you stalk her explicit locations of desire, keeping one eye always open. she creeps up on your laziest fears, the ones she hid for you in skyscrapers in 1989. together you see peacock blue quite often, sun rising over second avenue, over abandoned school-buildings. the ghosts get out just in time, avoid squinting in the glare. bleary-eyed merchants greet the day. if the city is a girl, she's a waitress, she's an actress. she has wrapped her legs around a variety of necks, sad-eyed men & women are attractive to her. she may hurt the ones she loves, but she's not going anywhere. she will never get jealous & leave you. you get to be the one to leave her, in charge of how many sirens, how much steam heat you can handle, how much money you can spend. she will always be there for you, with her unhealthy birds & secret gardens.

yet away from her you prosper. delight in being the only one on the block to let your lawn overgrow. behold the sky as clouds meander across. you are the name of a waitress. you are the new york times. you have dropped out of nothing. you haven't left anything. by leaving you have visited places where many people in new york are from. you huddle in the corner of a bookstore reading criticism with some inside information: how close you came to living at 101 st. mark's place, the building where it still says notley/berrigan on the #12A mailbox. if you had lived there, you might still be married, still share a private language, still help each other break through the armature of impossible evenings.

laughing drifting leaving. for example you left. before anybody you knew could really die. still there are significant souls to keep tabs on, by leaving & coming back. you are looking for a girl you used to know. she's an uncommon sort. curly-haired & curious. when you find her, she will have changed. you will try to explain to her what it used to feel like driving fdr drive after being away for a while, traveling other cities but still living in hers, you could hear her singing you home. you will try to explain what it will feel like today, driving down the west side highway, sick with anxiety & pretending to feel normal, chewing cinnamon gum & wondering what you are going to say to people. it seems if you don't live there, you haven't a leg to stand on. there's this mixed feeling of nausea & belonging. you'll bang your head against old doors, get marked by pleasant recognition & the sores of refusals. you'll remember loving & hating the city, or certain things about it. a street of delight, a street of terror, same street. you had a dream about that street. it didn't change the way you felt, it didn't change what you did. you left. you ate you wrote you fucked you slept. & now you are taking the george washington bridge into manhattan. if the city is a girl, you have loved her & lost her.

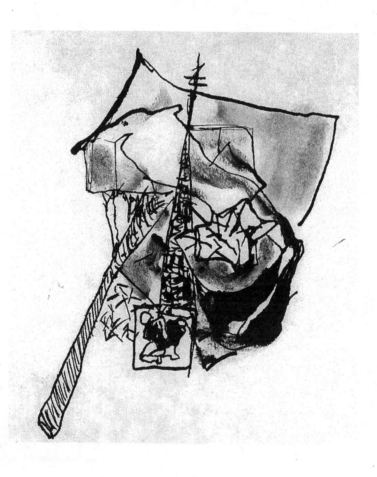

diner tables, winter

pools of molasses greet rivers of spilled creamers
ice patches on the sidewalk covered with wet leaves
tight necklines arresting necks, girl in a snowflake sweater

escaping all grey cars by crouching under steeples
then wandering in & shaking off her hair
water droplets kissing the floor
moisture hissing on air

the sounds of remembering, of thin poets wondering
if there were truth in the place where the axe fell
if there were guard rails to catch the falling

when drunk every night was a respite
when the politics of love were a choice
genius was sure as a snowplow
decision an icicle hanging

last of the cognac

for awhile it was in all of the poems
it tasted like candy like a bursting spring flower
in napa california on a front lawn
it tasted like jesus, it tasted like lettuce
it made us pause, then pounce, then pause

so with a piece of my dress i clean out the goblet
for the last of the cognac, it is like drinking jewelry
in a surrealist movie, the scents are tremendous
i am a painting in the lobby of a hotel
i become liquid carpet, i change

i jump at a knock at the door
at the disruption of sorcery on tender places
& i offer them petals all sewn up
eyes closed so i can't see the papers

the thaw

the thaw comes when you are not looking in an unlikely place inside
yourself. snowy patches are the residue of storms, deteriorating like
the black & flaccid tiles of the crumbling kitchen floor. somebody's
grey mercedes is just outside the door. all night the planes fly over.
people rarely mistake them for spaceships anymore, but sometimes
they do, thinking the lights are mysterious & definitely not like a
plane. planes flying low shake snow off of trees, cars climb steep &
dangerous inclines, the streets are awash with liquid history. now we
know why the squirrels were scurrying. why the squirrels were so
everywhere we couldn't help writing about them in our journals.
they had to store it up, all the nuts. Q: what does it snow for if it is
only going to melt? A: precipitation is a process that waters the
earth. & you couldn't think to say ah yes the snow falls how very
lovely the snow. a frozen nectarine on the porch, critters in the trash.
they leave footprints as evidence to the nature of the critter. there's
a few leaves left, the wind is their dance. there's a reservoir that feels
like england. you go there to relieve your stress. the stress of the
indoors to the rising lionness.

comfortable

in the park today
a hippie hopped the fence
fresh grass his reward

wouldn't it be lovely
just to sit around all day
living

poets and players, but not thieves
in new york there's fires &
in prairies there's dust

eventually i'll wind up in the bayou
mississippi where my porch comes from
writing poems for people

lying in pajamas i am
comfortable now
waiting to see what comes

1431 st. james court (a prophecy)

red brick hallelujia building 3 floors & a porch
& a fountain. a fireplace & a porch swing
where a man had a heart attack. symbols of the
grave, sleepy partiers, kitchen the size of
omaha. candelabra doorways, the ability to
make yourself small, like alice, wandering a
dangerous alley, amongst streets where cars are
not allowed. putting the old furniture into a
brand new place can be disconcerting, but it's
familiar after moving enough times. scraps of
paper get worn from carrying them around. a
pleasant jam resides on a poor piece of bread.
leaves leaden & heavy with moisture, i can
hear them heaving their drips.
i drag garlic out of my pores by sweating. i
encourage a masseuse; i haven't met her yet. i
yawn at lawrence ferlinghetti, fixate on the
moon. i don't speak italian, but the romance
languages betray each other. there is barely a
language you could hide from me in. i speak
eyelash anyway, & most people have some.
they fly in the wind as the body corrodes.
decays itself toward ashes with the help of a
heat lamp. the coronary artery keeps pumping
but the skin erodes, explosions. it contributes
to the world's debris, along with muffin tins, &
rosaries.
we will do our part to educate, to turn each
other on, turn pages, hold hands on saturdays,
swing lanterns in the yard. the sun room has a
kitchenlike linoleum, but with a love-potion-
stained rug placed down & a bit of iodine,
divine! we will make mortars & secure the
windows with chicago plastics for the winter.
we will escape the plagues & devour each
other before a cozy fire. there is nothing so
smooth as the future. there could be tire
swings in tunnels beneath excited feet.

kentucky derby 1996

thunderstorms speak sharply to the trees & to me. walking tall &
heavy lidded i find myself against a pole, slumped & unbecoming,
arms outstretched fending off memory. i can see them from blocks
away: derbies past. others in the vicinity are scanning the scene. like
hidden driveways, with their capacity for surprise, there are memo-
ries of parties, there are reunions & gold mines, dead batteries, dusty
road signs.

what i am seeing in the leaves of mint is oils & teething infants,
black beauties circling muddy tracks & high falootin' ladies clutch-
ing hats to blustery chests. what i am seeing in the leaves of mint is
crushing ice & lovers seething, wringing hands in isolated bedrooms.
their clarity of vision comes later, they hope, with skills acquired in
sleep. they have counties named after them, jessamine & woodford.
their shotgun thoughts are flashbacks, are porch games for the able-
minded. just like me they are wondering if every year, the year
before will be missing.

ky worksong

there goes someone
with an excellent shovel
finding importance
in being a recluse
as a daily ritual
"my work is really
my play!"
not shapeless employment
lining up rows
of glasses & cups like
the years before taking
glass stories to press
back to square one
near bear grass creek
washing the windows
with ammonia & water
fingerprints on the edge
of a rusty nail
& other drinks
red apple, russian bear
cherry sling, white rose
garnished with a peach slice
& the dirtiness of a daughter
introspective after
red ink bad luck
at the racetrack
all are led by their trotters
to their troughs

after work (mixed miracles of liquor & weather)

too much fancy bourbon over quaint ice cubes
is where i want to find myself after all that gibberish

i swept up the mess & now it's over
i know how to do it, use a mop or something

fetching umbrellas from the river of debris
good grownups crying the tears of unshed genius

a distant sky-cough, bleeping warning on the television
rain is all that water, landing on something loud

march thirty night

we've still got our coats on. we're still wearing easter dresses. the handle of the kettle's made that burning smell again. it smells like burned plastic, which it is. a mark on the wall makes me turn my head. i don't usually sit at this wall in particular. tea is too hot to drink. i am thirsty & eager but i know it's too soon. we found foil eggs resembling lavender flowers hidden under & around the roots of the trees. things we buried in actual dirt, trowelless, it was so soft the earth. sleeping is the so soft & only importance & afternoons in beds one of ours we get drunk on comfort, lost to the naps & the netherworlds. still in our easter dresses with hairdos that wear out & have to come down & be still underneath hats. wrists crack in the morning as i'm tying up my hair. i make mistakes throughout the day posture included. my coat's come off. her coat has a velvet collar. there is less steam. life cools & i don't know what's buzzing. what's careful. the hum of machines like a baby's gurgling stomach. still got my easter dress on, & shoes & socks & all that. still this hill of beans up here on my high horse where the road gets rusty & i end up home, tamed by what i can see. she's got a book in her hand but it doesn't look like it's going too well. she's got her easter dress off. how this floor makes me feel & these walls, how they make me feel bad. or how i feel good in spite of them or how i feel bad anyway. the dirty dishes & the fan is spinning & why all the spinning, why brains. furrowed brow, new hat (off), old dreams dirty wishes strained tree root for the throat. still got my easter dress on. hair down hands tied, age-old elixirs & a gathering of the mind. a robin's-egg-blue sweater. a twitchy foot. on/off.

so hard the wind blew she found windows

plastic garbage cans bouncing down the street
grey-violet ashes spilled from last season's barbecues

willow aunts are blowing

shuck the peeling paint
hail an umpteenth cloud
pull off the caulk

she will paint racehorses on the windows
she will paint babies on the windows

then spend the evening with a good game of pool
tall whiskey sours, two cherries, stems tied

architecture of the watershed

we've become two bottles in bed
two tailbones of a tantrum
the whimpery weeping
after the fight dies out

wet-mouthed with discretion
embroidered upon a calendar
lovely days together
naked marriage four-poster

still i claim speediness & suddenness
among the tricks left in the bag
i can still ignite this mythic hideaway
with jasmine & dark chocolates

my mind is racing faster than a train
instead i might inebriate the rain

for i am insistent upon ink
an imperative of faith
towers taller than light
& built on words

'a garden walk with lipstick' becomes
'dancing past the ivory boulevard'

& then crop up the killjoys
as we step up on stage
to serenade the sinners
the transition will not be smooth

sing o ancient voices
of my debonair options
as they come out my mouth
unconvincingly

II. gypsying

on a rail

you know that i'm not biting
i am not the road perverting
your passion for a foreign means
of travel

by the way i seem excited
i am the well, unstolen prose
cascading into this present
this moment of holy motion

this piece of track ferocious
& i do not deign
to ponder the blue-eyed warden
or the goddess of this dark region

you begin to tell me often
heaven is only a ride
heaven is us, & those around us
needing help & persistence

in their damaged floating glory holes
their oceans of wrong direction
friends in the peach trees of collusion
banging foreheads on the bark

like merry countrymen
horizon lines ever after
will be listening to this type
of question

how the bones howl
when you try to keep
your heart whole, your hair
cut up in a bowl

suicide of the brilliants

they made a mistake
maybe they come back
in the form of a cat
wander around kansas city

maybe they're in deers running
4 or 5 of them
running from the man

snow begins
ends a second later

maybe they're in the pattern of a plow
generations of concentration
the weather, then washing off in a pond

not able to make any improvements
weak & watery in some senses

they're the slender & elegant weeds
a quiet child needing a wagon
to carry her rocks around

they're in the small way she falls asleep
good in her mansion

such a lovely name for such a paltry girl
she's like the wrong side of branches
& so the mystery dies

ways to climb out
worn-out options
lost flakes, clear plastic wings
stuck to a fence, lifeless, just garbage

short tour before x-mas

just trying to fly before the snow falls
countdown to no parcel of leaves
short rites of passage inside of vans
full of fleeting genius, & amaranth
december's caravan is stark
through trees & hollows
pennsylvania ditches
genuine creeks & gulches
groggy in the instance of morning for cases
of beer split up the night before
mixed-up amigos, new friends, fred, etc.
combobulating separately
into one mighty blood spot
there's no blossoms left
no roadside attractions
in between cities where the music ends up
rhythmic prowess the influence
of the people powerfully affected
in the days when they went gypsying
children of great worth & beauty
not idlers

outlaws & lawbreakers

you can get arrested for wearing a diaper
you get to be a trash-picker instead of imprisonment
wearing a bright orange jacket that makes you visible
you get to use a pointy stick

waterbury plumbing & heating supplies
american anaconda amber brass company
lots of rivers are called "snake river"
if you don't like it build your own church

squirrels go nesting in their roosts
do hopeful capers involving nuts
as the sun goes down on your working
afternoon early this time of year

you can peer down easily into a ravine
catch a glimpse of a barrel being tossed
into the susquehanna river, it feels free
like a walk down the road

what kind of bird flies over atlanta wire

we were wolverines in the night
walls the color of pickle
making love in the weight room
fluid ounces of still small anthems
floating over our gorgeous nightmares

awaking to the sounds of the
soldiers of aluminum recycling
mentally we dress them in tortillas
as a holy order of repercussion for thieves
thieves of wisdom & coats, self-righteous polecats

then we with a broken windshield wiper
2 black jackets from 2 pot smokers
removed in cold-blooded georgia
in the light of day we stand
like farmers in a frozen cotton field

speaking to the cash crop
to the rain drop, then we wither
we feel like a gesture, set in motion
driving past needle buildings
injecting ill will, set apart

san francisco, january first

good god it's morning
& the queens of alleviation
clutch their vials
all over town

last night in taxicabs
the drivers sent mixed messages
did they like driving us around
or not?

now rain leaks onto bathroom tiles
magazines on the floor crinkle
into the new year's hat of cellophane

sleeping angel baby, banging her head against a dark dream
against my drunkenness, & when my memory goes
i'll still remember she is 24, she is the age of my love

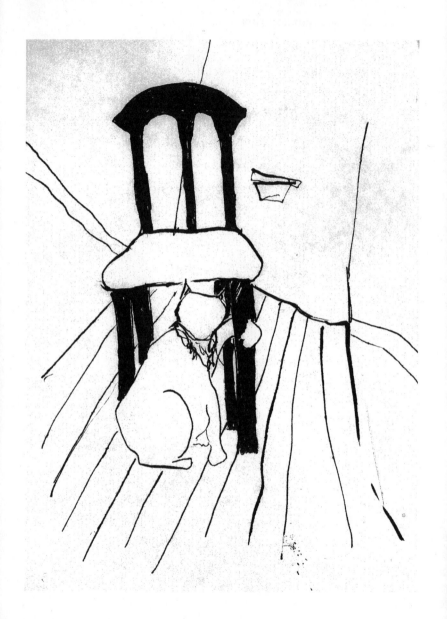

venice, california

cowgirl shirt
feathery holding
of cats onto legs of chairs
then knocking over lamps with confidence
in the clear & literal world

you get what you want by waiting
cough syrup helps
enjoy the sunshine

slats wood floors using eyes
& the vending machine all out

all white cats lying around & breathing
the mail falls in with the morning
the landlady hands you an envelope
& you climb the stairs
imbued with an understanding

what you make can tend to be insolent
what you forget is a path you got off

III. many's a pretty lady

balconys

ringing in the ears on a sunday at midnight. weight of the hands on the chest as the best solace. first chills of the season, and i sense a great shift. not one i haven't seen before, but in a different form. more smoke indicating a bigger, perhaps a brighter fire.

something is waiting on the horizon. yes i saw the sky tonight. it found me, i did not need to beckon it. yet it took me twice around the block to decide. driving while balancing the coffee cup. but i visited. i took puffs on a balcony with the risk of being locked out and a girl.

i do not hesitate to subject myself to pains. i could live in a dirty city. i could live poorly. i could walk from river to river. perpetuate uncertainty. spend hours with a girl holding cotton sweaters to her breast. wear too-small leathers walk beer-sticky floors. library afternoons on cold marble steps in memory.

and if there were not hands, if one evening found mine perfectly frozen. and if there were not voices, if the fear had made me irreparably mute. if no literature could be found on sidewalks, if no spicy words could be blended by walking feet. then i would have lived, and could still refer back.

once i built a chamber out of light and stone, along with some pepper and some lukewarm water. i would enter nightly and watch out the window and write in pencil. i wore pale green and knew that things had changed with the arrival of rains. saw people walk up an uneven stone path. some of them were students. some of them were friends. i tried to keep my bones from bursting through my skins. i saved a cow skull underneath a desk. i saved a few lives which in return saved mine. i speculated and drank liquids and built a foundation for futures, which are happening today in basements, on balconies.

what is waiting might only be me, or winter. it might also be a new way of doing, or an old way. the white capsules of invention have been swallowed. ink stains on the skin do tell. the most sliver of a moon rises over indian hill, and still it is greater than my thumbnail. inevitably, i walk across a field.

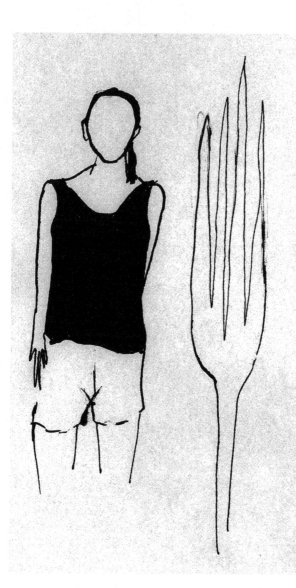

eileen dream #17

she was cleaning the kitchen
making poems out of the kitchen
i was making poems
out of watching her clean

she put silverware in a blue
tampax box, forks sticking out

i was watching her clean
talking to her kitchen
she was nervous is why
she was cleaning so feverishly

the kitchen table caught fire
pieces of furniture had been
catching fire recently
i took a walk

in the park, my arms pulled out
of the sleeves of my t-shirt
& wrapped around my stomach

she was making orderly the food
& dishes. she smelled like
berkeley, she was alive

this strange x

this girl had a boyfriend, she was tired
of him, he was away, it was a chilling

& depressing rain. we met outside the bar,
the bar was just closing, we sipped slushy

budweisers, fingers tucked up under
sweater sleeves & water-resistant jackets.

she sniffed her apartment like a kitten,
shooed the boys away like flies, secured me places;

a bed & for clothes to dry. i found postcards
on the floor from undesirables, like her

boyfriend, or mine, what i thought at the time,
didn't matter, she rolled like an otter,

pounced like a fox, invited me to mexico
for christmas, hollow bed talk.

this girl had a girlfriend, an affection
for polaroids, she said 'you just can't get

ecstasy like we used to get back in texas
where i first had sex.' her pillows were

white, we caught them on fire, her
girlfriend was gone, her white cats

applauded, & vines climbed the walls.
we waitressed together, & fooled all

the workers, & wrote secret letters,
ended friends & much better.

stephanie rose

she used to spend a lot of time
trying to decide if she was a good girl
or a bad girl, what it meant to be good
what it meant to be bad, & which
she was going to be

she makes me think of rose the flower
the dark-haired sentinel
negative space of a moonbeam

she asked me what i thought
& i said good girls, bad girls
fleshy earthlings all
i find them wry & exciting
watch them take off their sneakers

& she just took to it, the scene behind the scene
i kept speaking while she slept, dreaming the forbidden
for a couple of hours down the road, the folded ribbon

alice #2

alice is in france, & here in the states anne
is alice. there's another alice someplace else,
there's an elsie someplace else also but in this
town we got anne. we had anne where i grew
up also but i'm talking this anne plus this alice
who is in france, although the other alice could
be in france also, i wouldn't know, because once
there was a light on between alice & me & it went
out. she kept on saving her cigarette butts in the
box & being mean to everybody but in a way i
loved her. & the other alice i love the way you
love when you've never met somebody. & now
since she is in france i most likely will not meet
her, & now that there are alices & annes everywhere
& all over, & now that i can confess i never knew
no elsie i just plain lied, & now that we are separate.
& annes & alices everywhere are just too hard to
touch, except in the mind, we are all expatriates,
& though we are not all in france, we can pretend.

eileen read 80 books

what do you do after you read 80 books i asked
take a bath she said
& then she put me in one
with bubbles in the university president's office

they questioned me
i assured them she was my teacher
while inside i was shaking my head
80 books, 80 books, will i ever read them

fourteen lines

tailing girls is something i used to do
and i don't do it anymore now that i'm
rather involved with a beautiful siren
adjacent to my crawlings and climbings she
joins my capillaries in their brilliant pump
and wooziness, alarmingly switching with
no warning. i listen to her for hours
edging around sounds she is musicianly
o tara, you're quite irish and insane in the good way
'cause i can detect these things, and you are calmer
now, you are serious and dedicated and delicious
even when you are not sleeping you are innocent
illustrious and right, holy and hopeful, holding
lovely breaths inside, letting them out in intervals

love poem (refrigerator magnet poem)

peach could crush my spring
take of frantic breast
hair did flood the lake
honey storm

IV. as well as i know how

1966 legenda (girls' school found poem)

there is an angel in me whom i am constantly shocking
if it hadn't been for the olives in the martinis
we would have starved to death
frostbiting in november

ambition: to understand life
ambition: to marry & raise a baker's dozen
ambition: to find a place to call my own
ambition: only the wind of the morning knows

one third of the lemon trio
one fourth of the westerly clan
pink notes from hockey camp
take this route through our paths

flunked another gym test
only ten pounds to go, neatsy-keen!
happiness the best of all life's creatures
get out of my cage, i can't see

ambition: to be the first female astronaut
ambition: to write as well as i know how
ambition: to be a united nations interpreter & world traveler
ambition: to have an apartment in greenwich village

already the problem class, we managed
to break the bird bath. cricket was
behind the map, in the wastepaper basket
in fact everywhere but in her seat

postman, paperboy, how do you spell that?
yes we may drink when we are 16
our wildest moment—a headless horse
our idle footprints, grinders & apple crisp

ambition: to be an airline hostess & see
every corner of this world & the next
ambition: to be what i want to be
when i marry my multimillionaire

we, the poets of '66, leave a roasted
skylark, grace & all, to any willing pioneers
in the realm of purple verbosity. we, kathie &
hoxsie, leave our problem to freud to analyze

always dropping books, late for latin again
every now & then my existence is justified
honest-to-buddha, i didn't *see* the tree. & my raccoon
coat i leave to no one, as i intend to take it with me

dream

the devil will kill you
& god will not like you
if you buy new clothes

unless they resemble pajamas
you had when you were small
faded, yellow, thin

don't pick up the money
dollar bills perfectly folded
tucked under earth pods

letting you know
they were obviously planted
squares of sod, an impacted path

listen as hard as you can
listen for god

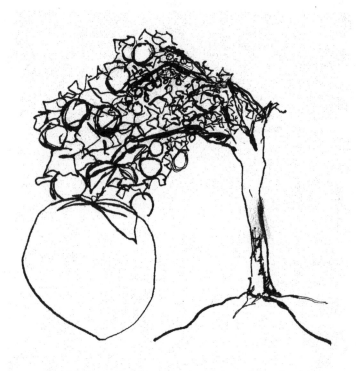

a fragile peach

say bruise first word
say achey button
hanging strutly & buxom
in tangles of love

say 'shave' & 'soft'
say fragrant & wily
say the fruit from each branch
falls hard from above

ripe arms around the green seed
dying to bloom like a volatile girl
taking a shower in the natural rain
too soon to fall prey too soon

outerplace

east of each moonbred bumpkin
lies a western star of idiom
ideology in reform

birds in greek music
levelling the playing field
trails of peninsula to follow

all grassy knolls sip quietly their gin
carbonated oceans bubbling

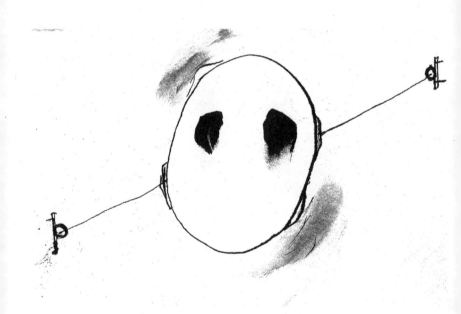

one thing's for sure

one thing's for sure you're smoking again
i have to drink 90 gallon carrot juice
i have to grind fresh pepper & bread
devise a calendar for your fair mischief
oh what heavy things these minds is for

in this poem #1

pulling my hat over my eyes in this poem
& smiling at ladies who make me embarrassed
& wanting more out of everything than it offers
& spending my youth dreaming of my death
of course i want to wake up tomorrow, sunshine

vision

someone just shook my eyes.
i didn't know i had shakeable eyes, or rather
i forgot i had them.

help me. help each other.

i think pajamas

i think pajamas are the best thing to wear
in your drawing class she takes off her clothes
in the bedroom i go to bed
in my nightmare i run from bunnies
you come to bed & i don't wake up
in the morning i wake up first
i think pajamas are the best thing to wear

yes i do want to run a hundred miles

i am thinking about diamonds
how they shine on demi moore
in her black cashmere sweaters
in her off-road vehicles

i wish i had diamonds worth $52
i don't bother to remember
what i wish

i keep falling back to catnap
is that ok?
i need a muffin
& a donut
& a job

how can she lie there sleeping?
ice melted in the night
& kept her up

i measure the weather
by my dream
about milk

i go buy some orange juice
& grape nuts & glance
at the tabloids surreptitiously

it looks good for the team
outside in warm rain

someday an important
meeting will greet me
i'll be running 40 miles

bernadette's reading (in the hollow bellowing of dark fall)

there's a little bird trapped in a skyway oasis
stand over there where it is
climb up on the ledge & try to free it

the little bird is very popular
it is very strange & mangy
give it a biscuit, it'll sing better

hang up the halo & help the moth out
like you helped the bird. hear the melody?
do you understand poetry now?

how it works is together
in a room is how it works
northeasterly is where's poetry
& they's gatherin'

if poetry is your gift, euphoric
in its practice, executive of its
witchery, strange & mangy ladies
& gentlemen, crawl out of the moats

wear long hair & linen pants
leeks & life & lined paper
crack candlelit walls clean open
bleed words inside stone walls once burned

lend me your leeches

it's like spending the night in a library
with milk ponies in a white tea pot
upstairs neighbors moving furniture
in every building all over town

a bit shaky standing in your house
next to hatched & unhatched poesy
like an open-mouthed boy
staring blandly at the sea

in the hard darkness, such mistakes
as charcoal, as bloodletting
as snake-charming matches
into light

trying to pen this mess this circus song & dance
this forest green winter between city & soft
the work of imps & toads lined up like arrows
in the house of trust

action in the ocean there's no clock
here, time is red liquid in a cup
it's squid as a part of dark pasta
it's drinking from the well of cretins

this great cloud of dust billows off diaries
covers my hands with messages & questions
manuscripts misplaced in history
versions in the jargon of virgins

hardback slippers on their eager feet
sounding like they just woke up
on christmas morning
thrown in direction of the breeze

you've lent me your house
i've shut the trembling window
sucked the poison out
house of trust

welcome to the morning, princess

in apricot balm & linty mischief
i awake in the crease of your soft arm
lovely in the white you never wear

trepidation of the day & its $50 decisions

i'm like catnip
an array of wild flowers
a radiator all scrambled
& making things cold

sometimes we come roses
last night we came diamonds

swollen buds, the missing link
the anastasia that walked into your life

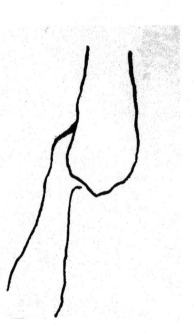

recommendation & information

exist & be happy
in the goodness of the deluge

all i have
are these damn documents

quit saying 'slipstream'

i have been in quiet ecstasy
holding your elbows

Cynthia Nelson is a poet and a musician. *The Kentucky Rules* is her third collection of poetry, after *Raven Days* and *Not Sisters* (with Maggie Nelson). Her musical projects include Retsin and Ruby Falls.

Tara Jane O'Neil is an artist and a musician. Her drawings and paintings have appeared on record covers and in aforementioned poetry books. Her musical projects include Retsin, The Sonora Pine, and an upcoming solo project.

New from Soft Skull Press

REPUBLICAN LIKE ME:
A Diary of My Presidential Campaign
by Sparrow
Available now

"All slaves freed, all debt forgiven" was his campaign promise. He unveiled shocking proof that Lincoln was a Marxist. How could Sparrow NOT have beaten Dole for the GOP nomination? Find out in *Republican Like Me*, the story of the vociferous and impassioned campaign trail of a revolutionary poet.

"One of the funniest men in Manhattan....Over and above everything else, Sparrow offers something to believe in."

—Robert Christgau
Village Voice

the haiku year

by Tom Gilroy, Anna Grace, Jim McKay, Douglas A. Martin, Grant Lee Phillips, Rick Roth, and Michael Stipe
Available now

"The beautifully designed *haiku year* consists of daily haiku written by a group of seven friends....There are some pretty awesome haiku here. Here's one: 'Before you could hang up/my machine caught/ a half-second of bar noise.'"

—*JANE* Magazine
August 1998

"The real revolution will begin when we all start communicating with each other with love, honesty and purity of heart—and this book is a three-line leap in that direction."

—Todd Colby

Soft Skull Press
98 Suffolk St. #3A • NYC • 10002

Distributed to the trade by Consortium Book Sales & Distribution, 1-800-283-3572
Access www.softskull.com for the latest Soft Skull catalog, text, and information.